The Five Critical Succession Conversations:
A Comprehensive Guide for the Family Business

To assess your business' succession readiness, an accompanying assessment could be found at www.successionstrength.com/assessment.

For bulk orders, contact us at info@successionstrength.com

First edition.

ISBN (Print): 978-1-7326109-0-3
ISBN (eBook): 978-1-7326109-1-0

The Five Critical Succession Conversations

A Comprehensive Guide for the Family Business

By Rochelle Clarke

Table of Contents

Introduction 6

Part One — How to Navigate This Book................................9

Navigation Guide...10

Part Two — The Conversations 15

Conversation One: The Foundation 16

    Scenario One: Are we a match? 18

Conversation Two: The Owner's Decision............................22

    Scenario Two: You are the successor; your area of expertise is
      similar to mine.. 24

    Scenario Three: You are the successor; your area of expertise
      is different from mine 26

    Scenario Four: You are not the successor; there is another role
      for you 29

    Scenario Five: You are not the successor; there is no
      other role for you... 31

    Scenario Six: You are not the successor; we will hire externally............. 33

    Scenario Seven: I am in the early stages of narrowing a wide field of
      potential successors 35

Conversation Three: The Successor's Decision 37

    Scenario Eight: I do not want to run the business; I am interested in
      having a role in it... 39

    Scenario Nine: I do not want to run the business; I am not interested in
      having a role in it... 41

Conversation Four: Performance 43

Scenario Ten: I am passing the business to multiple successors, each with a substantial role...45

Scenario Eleven: I need more support in this new role. 47

Scenario Twelve: I have little freedom to execute because of your presence 48

Scenario Thirteen: You (successor) are underperforming 50

Scenario Fourteen: We need to innovate or the business will suffer......52

Scenario Fifteen: Your new vision will kill my business............54

Scenario Sixteen: This business is taking over my life................56

Conversation Five: The Exit...58

Scenario Seventeen: I am selling the business.............................60

Scenario Eighteen: You should sell the business.........................61

Conclusion 62

Our Framework..63

About The Author 64

Want more? 65

Introduction

"Good morning; this is 57665, how may I help you?" the slightly nasal, imitation secretary voice inquired before the phone could ring a third time. Always before the third ring.

This is not the typical greeting that you would expect to come from the mouth of a seven-year-old, but, in our household, we all answered the business phone professionally. My parents are both veterinarians. My mother owned and ran the local animal clinic, while my father lent his expertise on an as-needed basis when larger livestock were involved. A critical point in my life, and subsequent career path, came in high school at the age of about thirteen; I, along with my peers, would choose the academic subjects we would concentrate on as a precursor to university studies and an eventual career in the selected area. My older brother chose science as a precursor to medicine and would volunteer or be invited to observe my parents as they treated animals. I was more interested in commercial pursuits and chose business.

My parents always gave us the freedom to choose our academic and career paths, so there was never the element of pressure. The family business supported us modestly as we progressed through high school and then moved on to university. One day, after my first year of university, I sat with my father to discuss how my studies were progressing and what my plans were for the future. I had done a few science courses during my first year of university—a time when, in American universities, your course exposure was a melting pot of subjects—and had done quite well in them.

"Dad, I will major in finance and international business," I declared. I did not realize it at the time, but this was another key marker in my career path.

"I am happy that you have decided," he responded, then added in a caring and advisory tone, "Remember that a business path is not something that your mother or I know much about, so we won't be able to guide you."

"Yes, Dad, I know that I will need to figure it out on my own," I responded with the ease and nonchalance of a naive teenager with the world in her hands.

Little did I know that by taking the freedom to make and follow through on that decision, I had essentially helped shutter our family business. Unfortunately, I wasn't the only one; before me, my brother chose to specialize in human medicine, and my younger siblings would follow in my footsteps and pursue business. With no viable heirs to continue the business, its fate as an ongoing enterprise in such a niche area was doomed.

***

This book is brought to you by Succession Strength, Inc. We believe that a succession transition could come from either a place of strength or a place of stress for all parties involved. Family businesses impact many employees around the globe and account for about 90% of revenues in the U.S. alone. Stressful successions could therefore negatively impact a very large number of persons.

To ensure a transition that is as smooth and stress-free as possible, our approach is built on three pillars—Communication, Preparation and Execution. Communication forms the basis of the entire process and runs throughout the Preparation and Execution phases. In our work, we have found a number of key conversations either missing, overlooked, or given too little attention in the succession process. Failure in these areas can result in a misalignment of objectives and unnecessary stress within the process that could eventually cause the collapse of the business.

For this reason, we focus in depth on the key conversations that should be had during the business succession process, both from the perspective of the business owner and the successor.

Communication can at times be difficult. If one considers how tricky it could be to maintain these skills in the regular world regardless of relationship ties, this challenge is magnified in family businesses where personal relationships provide a potentially more complicating dynamic. We believe that every family business should have in its arsenal the tools to have good, effective conversations that lead to outcomes that will ultimately advance the business and enable smooth transitions.

Parties should dedicate time to establishing the personal and logistical **foundation** for the succession. Afterwards, both the owner and the intended successor should clearly indicate their **decision** to either enter into the transition or not. In the beginning phases of a transition, communication with key stakeholders is important for as smooth a start as possible. Eventually though, as business operations progress, tough **performance**-related conversations may be needed. Then, finally, if things are not heading in the intended direction, it may be necessary to have a conversation to **exit** the business altogether.

In all, our work has shown that there are five critical areas that every family business should be equipped to address. Conversations in these areas (the Foundation, the Owner's Decision, the Successor's Decision and Performance Management) can pave the way for a successful business transition. In the undesired situation of a permanent exit from the business, families should also be empowered to handle the Exit effectively.

Happy reading!
Rochelle

Part One—How to Navigate This Book

No matter where you are on your journey of business succession, this book provides you with the tools needed to make it a success. The accompanying survey at www.successionstrength.com/assessment could help evaluate the effectiveness of your business' succession communication.

To make it user friendly, in Part One of *The Five Critical Succession Conversations: A Comprehensive Guide for the Family Business* we have detailed a summary of each key conversation: the Foundation, the Owner's Decision, the Successor's Decision, Performance Management, and the Exit. Under each of these, we have included the potential scenarios that you may face, with perspectives from both the owner and the successor. We understand that every business is different, so we have gone one step further and highlighted key areas you will need to consider when having these conversations.

The word owner, when it appears, is used to refer to the existing business owner. Because we recognize the role of either gender as a viable business leader, we have varied the use of relevant gender pronouns (he, she, his, her).

Whether you are just beginning to plan for your business' succession or are navigating a complicated situation that has already arisen, simply read Part One to discover the most relevant scenario for you and your business. *The Five Critical Succession Conversations: A Comprehensive Guide for the Family Business* does not need to be read in sequence; each section provides general principles of communication that can assist in making your transition as seamless as possible. Assess your communication strength at www.successions trength.com/assessment before, during or after completing the book.

Navigation Guide

Conversation One: The Foundation

Like a marriage, determining the compatibility of the parties is critical for a successful union. This chapter describes the initial conversation that needs to happen between the current owner and the intended successor to gauge whether their desires are aligned. It lays the foundation for the succession journey.

Scenario One: Are we a match?
1. To what degree is there interest in the business?
2. How can we authentically discuss this in a way that strengthens our relationship?

Conversation Two: The Owner's Decision

Tactfully communicating the decision of who will manage the business going forward without any ambiguity is crucial. This chapter guides the owner through the task of revealing his decision and covers every likely scenario that could be navigated.

Scenario Two: You are the successor; your area of expertise is similar to mine.
1. How much resistance should be expected?
2. What new role(s), if any, will the owner now assume?

Scenario Three: You are the successor; your area of expertise is different from mine.
1. If both owner and new successor are working in the business after the decision has been communicated, who is in charge?
2. What should we do if additional expertise is required?
3. When should full control be handed over to the successor?

Scenario Four: You are not the successor; there is another role for you.
1. How do we manage negative feelings of an individual who is assigned a lower position in the company than they would like?
2. How do we manage the relationship between the successor and person who was not selected?

3. How can the person who was not selected still receive opportunities for advancement within the organization?

Scenario Five: You are not the successor; there is no other role for you.
1. How do we preserve a positive relationship between the owner and the individual?
2. How can the owner support this individual in their pursuit of a new career outside the company?
3. How can we work together to create a positive story around the succession decision?

Scenario Six: You are not the successor; we will hire externally.
1. Do the rejected individual's feelings pose any risk to the business?
2. What are the best options for the individual's role going forward?

Scenario Seven: I am in the early stages of narrowing a wide field of potential successors.
1. How do I fairly involve all interested successors regardless of how close I am to each?
2. How do I select the next owner from multiple potential successors?
3. How to deal with conflict among successors?
4. How do I deal with unqualified or underqualified successors?

Chapter Three: The Successor's Decision
Deciding whether to lead a company is life-changing; not only for the successor but also for everyone invested in the business. This chapter provides tools for clearly articulating the decision while managing the expectations and sensitivities of all stakeholders in the business, including the owner.

Scenario Eight: I do not want to run the business; I am interested in having a role in it.
1. How do we preserve our relationship, and keep the door open for incumbency at a later time?
2. How do we handle a potential successor who is only interested in low responsibility positions?
3. What do we do if company problems prevent this individual from wanting the role?

Scenario Nine: I do not want to run the business; I am not interested in having a role in it.

1. How do we deal with conflicting views on the desirability of running the business?
2. How can the individual's business decision not jeopardize the family relationship?
3. How do we deal with potential impact of scandal at the decision not to run the company?

Chapter Four: Performance

The transition of owner to successor must be smooth, as drops in business or personal performance can quickly have a devastating impact. This chapter arms both the successor and owner with tools to manage this reality.

Scenario Ten: I am passing the business to multiple successors, each with a substantial role.

1. How do I manage successors who follow our traditional operations versus those who want to innovate?
2. How should equity be allocated to successors who, temporarily, cannot contribute as much as initially agreed?
3. How should I guide successors on handling informal channels of communication within the business?

Scenario Eleven: I need more support in this new role.

1. How do I navigate informal channels that may be hurting my efforts?
2. How can I be taken more seriously in this new role?
3. How do I get help identifying gaps in my knowledge or skills?
4. How do I overcome imposter syndrome or real under-qualification for this role?

Scenario Twelve: I have little freedom to execute because of your presence.

1. How can I make the past owner aware of his/her restrictive presence?
2. How can I stop the past owner making decisions that are the successor's to make?
3. How can I stop the past owner from undermining the successor to key stakeholders?

Scenario Thirteen: You (successor) are underperforming.
1. What should we do when key stakeholders are unhappy with the successor?
2. What should we do when business operations are suffering?
3. What should we do when sales are suffering?

Scenario Fourteen: We need to innovate or the business will suffer.
1. How do we innovate but still protect our heritage?
2. How do we introduce innovation into a business that is not broken?
3. How do we agree on the acceptable amount of risk involved with the innovation?
4. How do we agree on areas that should not be changed?

Scenario Fifteen: Your new vision will kill my business.
1. What might be the successor's motivations for changing how things are done?
2. How do we deal with sensitivities the owner may have regarding their legacy?
3. To what extent should the successor be given creative freedom?

Scenario Sixteen: This business is taking over my life.
1. How do I let the owner know that I am feeling overwhelmed by family overexposure?
2. How do I address intrusive behavior from other family members?
3. As a family, how do we work together to create balance between work and our personal lives?

Chapter Five: The Exit
Deciding to sell or close the family business is an emotional, but sometimes necessary reality to plan for. Whether motivated by the owner or other stakeholders, this chapter provides practical tools to handle the necessary conversations with tact and empathy while achieving results.

Scenario Seventeen: I am selling the business.
1. How do we deal with the emotional impact of this decision on the family?

2. How do we go about the sale while considering its potential impact on the family, workforce, and community?
3. How do we know if selling is the best option?

Scenario Eighteen: You should sell the business.

1. Is selling really the best option?
2. How do we involve the owner in the sale process?
3. How do we weigh the owner's wishes against those of the stakeholder(s) in the sale process?

Part Two—The Conversations

Chapter One: The Foundation

I reflected on my own family business story as I visited my neighbourhood florist, an older gentleman in his early seventies who had the most pleasant demeanour and smile as he manned the phones and processed orders. I visited his flower shop frequently in the years that I lived in the city. Having met most of his family in that time, I was puzzled.

"Mr. Shaw," I asked, "do you have any children? I haven't seen them around."

"Oh, yes!" he boomed with his big smile. "I have a son who is forty-two, another who is thirty-nine, one who is nineteen, and a lovely daughter who is ten. The boys have no interest in the business, but the girl, she really likes flowers. She will take over the business."

I nodded and smiled politely. A quick glance at the incredulous look on the face of his long-time assistant echoed my thoughts . . . That desire would, sadly, be unlikely to materialize

***

The Foundation Conversation

When beginning the planning process of succession in a family business, several things need to be considered. The owner must appraise the situation: who is the ideal successor? Do they want the role and are they suited to it? What are the implications of my choice? Potential successors must also be mindful: am I suited to this role? Am I willing and able to perform? Does my vision for the company align with the owner's?

It is critical to lay a foundation of clear communication and mutual understanding in order to develop a plan for succession that works for all parties. In this chapter, we explore the importance of choosing the correct successor and managing this conversation.

Key conversation discussed in this chapter:

- **Scenario One:** Are we a match?

Scenario One: Are we a match?

While a job may be a full-time commitment, running a business is an *over-time* commitment. Let us compare it to one form of commitment that is universally touted as the bellwether of commitments— marriage. A lot of time and effort is spent on the planning stages of a marriage: from creating the wish list of partner attributes; to dating until the partner with the best potential is found; to formalizing the intent to commit with an engagement; and finally, sealing the deal with the signing of the marriage certificate.

The irony is that the amount of time that a couple spends actively working on their marriage is way less than the amount of time a business owner spends working in and on his or her business. In most cases, a married couple may spend on average about ten to twelve hours a day in each other's presence (including time spent asleep) if one or both work outside the home. A business owner could spend anywhere from eight to ten hours working in the business and countless hours strategizing or handling other business related issues outside of normal work hours; when your name is on the door, you do not have the luxury of taking a mental break. The survival of the business literally depends on you.

Incredibly, for an activity that is so important and occupies so much of the business owner's life, many successors do not receive the level of wooing and validation required to ensure an alignment of values and direction before entering into such a major commitment. According to PricewaterhouseCoopers's (PwC) U.S. New Vines from Strong Roots: Family Business Survey 2016/2017[1], and consistent with prior surveys, the number one form of expected ownership change for family businesses is via transition to the next generation to own and run.. However, many family businesses fail as a result of improperly managed succession. PwC's survey highlighted that 43% of businesses have no succession plan in place.

The first step in a succession should be to open a dialogue between the current owner/CEO and the intended successor. The seeds of succession are

---

[1] PricewaterhouseCoopers South Africa, "New Vines from Strong Roots: Family Business Survey 2016/2017", South African Edition, South Africa: 2016, https://www.pwc.co.za/en/publications/family-business-survey.html

sown in this conversation where the owner leader invites a potential successor to a meeting to gauge interest, passion, and aptitude.

Why is this conversation so important?

We all carry assumptions about the people in our lives and presume to understand, to some degree, what they think and want. However, if we do not take the time to verify the accuracy of our assumptions, we are likely to find ourselves facing difficult and unexpected situations, especially during times of change. This is especially true when a business is involved.

The day to day needs of the business prevents many owners from proactively engaging in these conversations. However, without a planned succession, the future of the business could be at stake. Employees, family members, and customers are put at risk without a clear bridge to the next generation. Significant conflict can arise within the family, severing relationships for generations if sons and daughters argue over roles and stake in the company. Most failed transitions are a result of a breakdown in communication within the family or inadequately prepared heirs. To maintain the health of the business and the strength of the family, senior leaders in family businesses should make succession conversations a top priority.

Even if the conversation took place informally years prior, when the successor comes of age, the conversation should be had again to confirm and align on the intentions of both parties. This is because plans that were first established when would-be heirs were young might likely no longer be as certain with the passage of time. What is more certain is that a person's personal and professional interests will change over time. An heir who may have expressed indifference towards the family business in their twenties could well discover a belated interest in it when they enter their thirties and forties.

In some families, members may find it difficult to express what they are really thinking due to cultural norms. However, it is important that explicit conversations about the future of the family business be had, and that these conversations encompass immediate as well as mid-term and long-term plans.

Taking over the reins of any business, particularly one that has been in existence for many years, requires time and unwavering dedication. Unless a successor consciously agrees to undertake this effort, he/she may not have the passion or motivation to remain committed to the effort when things do not go as smoothly.

By having this conversation, the company puts at ease any concerns in the minds of key stakeholders about the business' continuity and longevity.

Agreements and arrangements in a family business are oftentimes made informally, with customer and vendor relationships founded on a handshake between people or groups with decades of personal history. It is important that the successor be allowed sufficient time to become familiar with nuances like these, which are essential to the operation of the business.

No business operates in a vacuum—business partners, customers and vendors are necessary for its continued success, and they need to feel secure about the future of the company that they in turn rely on. As founders mature and begin to delegate more responsibilities to their heirs, they need to keep track of precisely who is in charge of what, and in what manner.

Management styles differ; the approach that the owner might have taken for a particular task may be very different from the approach of the successor. Conversations between the owner and successor about the transition need to be thorough, accounting not only for the period of transition, but also anticipating what will happen post-transition.

Initial succession planning discussions mark only the beginning of a long series of conversations that will need to continue into the future.

What could happen if this conversation does not take place?

If this conversation does not take place, the business may continue built on a number of unfounded assumptions. However, if these assumptions prove incorrect, the existence of the business may be threatened and family relationships could suffer. For example, the current owner of a particular business may find out too late that the person he/she had in mind as the likely successor has decided to follow a another career path. Likewise, a potential successor may feel slighted at not being asked to succeed their predecessor and may cause drama within the family.

Ultimately, such misunderstandings reduce the amount of time for a smooth transition with the right successor and may result in diminished confidence from other employees, customers and/or vendors.

<u>When is the best time for the conversation to take place?</u>

This series of conversations should begin as early as possible to allow sufficient time to prepare for and execute the transition. It could be initiated be either the current owner or one of the likely successors.

Some primary factors that can dictate the timing of the foundation conversation are:

- The amount of time that the current owner intends to remain in control of the business (may be dictated by age and/or health); and
- The time at which a potential successor is identified by the owner or self-identifies to the owner.

In addition, several factors may add urgency to the conversation, such as the complexity of the business' operations, and the amount of time that is available and/or expected to be needed for the successor to become proficient. With some family businesses it can take years, if not decades, for the successor to be completely prepared to assume the full scope of responsibilities deferred in the succession. Quite often the owner has especially strong opinions about the way that the company should be managed, in which case the transition process should begin even earlier and follow a more gradual process.

One final consideration dictates the timing for the succession conversation: whether or not a suitable successor even exists. For example, when there is no one in the family who is interested in or capable of assuming the responsibility, the owner might have to reaching beyond the immediate family circle and look externally in the search for a successor. This type of conversation is implicitly more complicated and likely to require multiple iterations.

Chapter Two: The Owner's Decision

Let's take the story of Peter and his family's third generation business—a local design house that specialized in the making of uniforms for companies. Founded by his grandfather, a storied tailor, and carried on by his mother—a popular designer in her own right—Peter had no relevant design skills to consider as his family pondered the business's succession. With an overseas tertiary degree in business operations, Peter also had no plans to have a role in the family business.

As fate would have it, an operations challenge in the family business resulted in his return to his home country to resolve the issue. During that time, his passion for the operations element of the business became more apparent. He and his mother discussed making his presence in the business more permanent.

However, a design house is nothing without a head designer. With the impending retirement of his mother, they jointly recognized that an external non-family member would need to fill the critical role of head designer. In preparation for that eventuality, Peter and his mother have taken the unconventional but practical approach of having him run the business from his seat in operations while she continues to design so that he would eventually be able to manage the hired designer.

***

Conversations about
The Owner's Decision

Once a successor has been selected, the current owner must have the appropriate conversations with relevant parties to ensure an environment of transparency and reduce any doubts that may call the continuity of the business into question. Managing expectations, setting boundaries and ensuring that relationships with key stakeholders are maintained remain crucial for the transition to succeed.

In this chapter, we provide a guide for the key scenarios the owner is likely to face after making his or her decision.

Key conversations discussed in this chapter:

- **Scenario Two:** You are the successor; your area of expertise is similar to mine.

- **Scenario Three:** You are the successor; your area of expertise is different from mine.

- **Scenario Four:** You are not the successor; there is another role for you.

- **Scenario Five:** You are not the successor; there is no other role for you.

- **Scenario Six:** You are not the successor; we will hire externally.

- **Scenario Seven:** I am in the early stages of narrowing a wide field of potential successors.

Scenario Two: You are the successor; your area of expertise is similar to mine

<u>Why is the key conversation so important?</u>

A successor is selected, and, at face value, this appears to be the easiest of potential transition scenarios. However, even if the owner and successor have similar interests and areas of expertise, conflicts can still arise due to issues such as different management styles, generational relationship patterns, etc. that could jeopardize the succession. It is critical to prepare not only the successor, but also key stakeholders, for this new dynamic.

Change will often create difficulties of one kind or another. A change in leadership can be especially challenging and/or confusing for the individuals who have routinely interacted with the owner in the past and who now need to learn to interact with his or her successor.

This conversation is one of the many guidance conversations that the owner should have with the successor.

<u>What could happen if the key conversation does not take place?</u>

Individuals who have routinely engaged with the owner in the past may change their behavior and responses when engaging with the successor. Issues that may not have required discussion in the past could suddenly become problematic simply because of a difference in style. Unexpected resistance and/or conflicts may arise from situations that the owner may have previously handled with ease. Ingrained behaviors like continuing to defer to the owner for guidance and second-guessing the successor's decisions can further undermine the successor's authority and erode both confidence in the decision and the ability of the successor to succeed.

Further, issues that may arise due to generational differences can be especially challenging. Decisions or processes that were accepted at face value when initiated by the owner may suddenly be doubted or questioned under the direction of a younger successor with less experience. Cascading differences of opinion can continue to arise as the confidence of everyone involved erodes. Rumors and stories expressing negative opinions of the successor can further degrade the situation to the point where the successor can no longer effectively lead.

When is the best time for the conversation to take place?

This one-on-one conversation should occur between the owner and successor just before the decision is made public. Afterwards, the owner should lead the campaign to notify and engage the successor and key stakeholders on the change.

Ideally, the owner, successor and all those with whom he or she will be engaged in ongoing business relationships, should discuss the change in leadership as soon as, or just before (depending on the priority of the relationship), the leadership decision is made public. It is essential for all expectations to be explicitly outlined. For example, if the owner has decided to give the successor final decision-making power, this must be explicitly stated. If the owner is retaining decision-making power in specific areas, these especially need to be clearly defined. Most importantly, once these decisions are finalized and announced, they must be executed without exception.

Scenario Three: You are the successor; your area of expertise is different from mine

<u>Why is this key conversation so important?</u>

As the successor assumes his role as the new person in charge, there will be inevitable changes of roles and relationships for other members of the business. This is particularly complex when the successor's area experience does not align with the owner's. Let us examine Peter's story at the beginning of this chapter. In that example, the outgoing owner was a design expert while the chosen successor, Peter, is an expert in operations. Staff may now have a different reporting structure and vendors may have to develop a new relationship. There would have previously been the natural blurring of functional and operational roles; in the past, staff would have approached Peter's mother for both design and business-related matters. Now, they would have to approach another head designer for the former, and Peter for the later.

The danger is in the details, specifically when it concerns understanding proper accountability. Functional responsibilities are rarely silos that can be managed without interconnectivity with other areas of responsibility. It is critical that the boundaries between major areas of responsibility are identified and roles and responsibilities clarified. This discussion and its outcomes must be communicated to the workforce, business partners, and even customers before changes in responsibilities are implemented. All of the individuals who will be impacted must be notified, the potential impact of the changes fully discussed, and the details worked out.

The movement of roles and responsibilities may also result in unanticipated outcomes that must be worked through. Even when the owner and successor make the initial determination that they have successfully divided responsibilities, upon further inspection, as in Peter's case, they may realize that there is a gap in functional leadership that neither of them has the willingness or ability to fill. This may require the hiring of an external person with the necessary skills. The insertion of an external person into the organization can be particularly stressful for many individuals and must be communicated with the correct attention to change management.

If possible, it would be beneficial to provide a timeline for the completion of the transition. This would allow all those individuals, both inside and outside the company, to adjust their expectations and to develop transition plans of their own.

Finally, even though responsibilities may be shared, there remains the unanswered question of who has ultimate decision-making responsibility when the owner still has an active role in the business. Who actually runs the company? This is a sensitive question. Its outcome defines the true hierarchical relationship between the owner and the successor. Though this question may be awkward to discuss, it is essential that there is clarity about who has final say about critical business decisions during the time of the transition and until the owner exits the business.

What could happen if the conversation does not take place?

Confusion and, with it, loss of confidence in the transition, can result if the details of the succession are not worked out and fully discussed with all impacted individuals. Without thorough, transparent and consistent communication, it is particularly in the gray areas at the boundaries of functional responsibilities that problems can arise. One party may assume that another is carrying out a task and vice versa with the result that the task is not performed.

Additionally, when there is a gap between the owner and the successor's skills that require the introduction of a third person, uncertainty and anxiety are likely compounded unless adequately communicated.

When this type of confusion occurs, business productivity and efficiency decreases. Mistakes could be made that result in poor service, and that increase costs related to correcting errors resulting from poor and/or conflicting communications between functional areas.

When is the best time for the conversation to take place?

While, ideally, all of these details should be discussed and agreed upon before the successor takes on his/her new role, realistically, many details will be missed until they come up in the actual work environment. Both the owner and the successor should be open about this in their communications with all relevant stakeholders. Provisions must be made in advance to provide a structure for resolving ambiguities and/or gaps in responsibility as they occur, and to communicate a satisfactory response to all those who are impacted.

Scenario Four: You are not the successor; there is another role for you

Why is this key conversation so important?

For various reasons, the owner and possible successor have reached the conclusion that he or she is not going to be selected to lead the business. An offer has been made to this individual to remain as part of the company but in another role. It is important to be clear about what this actually means, both from the perspective of the owner and that of the individual. There are three possible outcomes that will require clarification in the near future.

The **first** outcome is that both the owner and the individual expect there to be a real possibility of additional advancement and leadership positions for the individual in the mid to long-term future. In this case, a long-term plan for advancement might be put in place that will allow the individual to gain the skills and experience required to take on more responsibility.

Second, the individual may be offered a position, but with the understanding that there will be no opportunities for advancement or expansion of that role in the future. In this case, either or both owner and this individual feel that he or she is fundamentally not suited for or uninterested in advancement. Indeed, it may be expected that this individual will leave the company at some time in the near future.

Finally, the owner may have some doubts about the person that he/she has selected to be successor. Perhaps the owner is concerned that the selected person will not stay with the company on a long-term basis, or perhaps he or she is concerned about the capabilities or leadership style of the selected person. The owner may feel the need to manage risk by having this 'rejected' successor serve as a back-up successor. Keeping the back-up successor in a position within the company would allow for easy transition in case the successor turns out to be unsuited to the leadership role.

What could happen if the conversation does not take place?

If the owner and the individual do not explicitly discuss the outcome that is most relevant to the situation, there may be differences of opinions that will inevitably result in conflict. For example, the owner may feel that he/she is giving this individual a position until they can find something outside the company that is more suited to their skills. The individual may have assumed, however, that taking this role would be an opportunity, or indeed an invitation, to gain skills and experience that will allow them to take on more responsibility on a long-term basis. If this difference of opinion is not resolved, the individual will come to feel bitter and rejected due to unfulfilled expectation. The owner, in turn, may resent the persistent requests for support from someone who he/she is expecting to leave the company. At worst, the individual may be fired but only after an ugly confrontation.

<u>When is the best time for the conversation to take place?</u>

These options should be discussed at the time a decision is made to choose a different successor but before the successor is formally announced. It is also likely that several follow-up conversations will be required to clarify the details of the arrangement and ensure compliance. Depending on the option and timing, the actual successor may be brought into the conversation and may be required to make the final decision about the long-term role of the individual.

Scenario Five: You are not the successor; there is no other role for you

<u>Why is this key conversation so important?</u>

This conversation is important for two reasons:

First, it provides closure between the owner and the individual who has been passed over. It allows both parties to express their feelings and, hopefully, conclude with a satisfactory relationship.

Second, it provides an opportunity to create a common, affirming, and progressive story between the owner, successor, and the non-selected individual. This is the public story that explains how the succession process took place and the reasons for its outcomes. The common story ensures that there is a smooth, uncontested transition for the successor and for the non-selected individual, who will now move into a different stage of his or her career.

<u>What could happen if the conversation does not take place?</u>

Without this shared and publicized story, individuals who are concerned or merely curious about the succession may fill the void with their own versions of what transpired or rationale for the final outcome. Once these fabricated half-truths become public, they will be difficult to dispel. Additionally, it is important on a private level for the business owner and the individual who has been passed over to reach an amicable settlement, especially since the family bond may be at stake. Life is a journey, and it is difficult to know what the future may hold. There may be a time in the future when with either the business owner or the new successor look to this individual for advice or support. Preserving all of these personal and professional relationships is therefore critical.

<u>When is the best time for the conversation to take place?</u>

The sequence of conversations between the business owner, the successor and individuals who were considered but not selected must occur in rapid succession and as much in private as possible. Once the decisions are agreed, then a common public announcement should be made immediately. This will minimize rumors and fabricated stories about the succession.

Scenario Six: You are not the successor; we will hire externally

<u>Why is this key conversation so important?</u>

Bringing an external successor into the company will be an enormous change for everyone involved. The external successor, despite the best preparation, will have numerous obstacles to overcome that a family-member successor would not. The external successor will need help navigating the company's culture in order to overcome these obstacles. Determining how this should be done and by whom is of vital importance. In addition, the conversation between the business owner and the non-selected family member(s) will be one of many that need to happen ahead of and in preparation for a successful transition of leadership to the external successor.

In this conversation, the business owner and the non-selected family member successor will need to clarify any unresolved questions or feelings between the two of them to ensure that they do not interfere with the transition. Additionally, it is important that they clarify the role of the non-selected family member(s). There are three options of future roles for the non-selected family member:

First, this individual may be asked to play a role as a strategic advisor to the external successor. The aim of this would be to assist the external successor in navigating both the business itself and the company culture. This may be a permanent or a temporary role. The successor may be expected to learn from the external person in order to assume a more prominent role in the future.

Second, there may be a role for this individual in the company going forward, but not in a strategic position or other position, that requires professional engagement with the external successor. This may be a role with lesser responsibility. The conversation will need to clarify where the family member's position in the company.

Finally, this individual may choose to leave the company altogether. This, too, will need to be clarified and an appropriate storyline crafted to ensure that the individual's exit does not cause difficulties for the transition of the business to the external successor.

Depending on the future role of the non-selected family member, it is possible that two transitions might occur in the business at the same time —the transition of incumbency to the external person, and the transition of the family member to his/her new role. These two transitions need to be carefully orchestrated.

What could happen if the conversation does not take place?

If this conversation does not take place, at the very least, there could be negative interactions and consequences during the external transition of leadership. Without the right level of assistance, the external successor may spend valuable weeks and months navigating the company culture at the expense of the business operations. Failure to enlist the non-selected family member in a supportive role could be a lost opportunity to ensure the company's success.

At its worst, failure to clarify the role of the non-selected family member could lead to confusion and ambiguous stories about the succession process. This, in turn, could lead to loss of trust in the external person and his/her failure to fully integrate into the company, which may have a negative impact on the company's operations and/or reputation.

When is the best time for the conversation to take place?

This conversation between business owner and non-selected family member should happen after the business owner has selected the external person, but before the selection results have been made public. It is important that this conversation occur after the external person is selected so that there is sufficient awareness of the potential transition needs of the external person. This will help determine the best role for the family member going forward.

Scenario Seven: I am in the early stages of narrowing a wide field of potential successors

<u>Why is this key conversation so important?</u>

Not all transitions from a business owner to a successor involve a single successor. Often in family businesses there are multiple potential successors. In the past, the task may have been as simple as selecting the oldest male heir. However, this is no longer the case in many cultures. It is now increasingly popular to have any of the business owner's children, as well as extended family, be eligible potential successors regardless of birth order or gender.

In this scenario, the potential successors have selected one of their compatriots to represent them in the early set of conversation(s) with the business owner. The business owner may not be as close to many of the potential successors and may not be intimately familiar with their role in or contributions to the business.

Ideally, as the field of successors in narrowed, the conversations will happen without the use of a representative. With a narrowed field of potential successors, all viable successors with relevant roles should have a seat at the table to discuss succession with the business owner but this may not be possible in the initial stages if there are many potential successors. The goal is to work out a provisional understanding of how the succession will occur. This conversation is important because it provides clarity around the transition process. It also circumvents any disagreements between family members which could significantly obstruct smooth business operations.

<u>What could happen if the conversation does not take place?</u>

If the details of a succession process involving multiple successors are resolved and clearly communicated, there is risk that various family members may disagree. Disagreements may result in in-fighting and attempts for control of a portion of company ownership. This process can be lengthy and invariably unpleasant for everyone involved, putting both the family and business relationships at risk.

Even if the potential successors are amicable, any disagreements or chaos surrounding how a business should be 'fairly' divided can bring a company to a standstill while the negotiations are had. Often in cases where there is no satisfactory resolution, the business ends up being sold and the profits divided among the successors.

<u>When is the best time for the conversation to take place?</u>

Defining a successor selection process, especially if one is not in laid out in a company charter or constitution can potentially be a long and complicated process that requires external assistance. For this reason, it should occur as many years as possible before the actual transition is to take place to allow for family members to have time to provide input, agree and be comfortable with the process.

In cases where none of the potential successors have the qualifications or experience to run the company, it is particularly important that this conversation take place many years before the transition to allow for development and preparation of a universally agreed plan to select an external party.

Chapter Three: The Successor's Decision

The Johnson family was well known and respected. They owned and operated the most popular chain of gift shops - a venture they continued to run for more than four decades. I sat down with the elder Mr. Johnson, the patriarch of the enterprise, as the transition to his children and eventual successors was in progress.

He explained that, out of a combination of necessity and intention, his children learned the business of operations at a young age; they helped with a variety of skill-appropriate tasks each year as they grew up. This, Mr. Johnson would explain, was to help them develop an ingrained passion for the business. While they did not all develop this passion, three of his five children eventually gravitated back to the family business.

Mr. Johnson had maintained unvoiced hope that they would carry on the business's legacy. Conversations around the role that that they would play in the business, however, did not happen until the children were young adults. The children initiated these conversations after they had pursued their passions externally and felt both the need and a sufficient level of empowerment to contribute to the building of the business.

Through an unwitting combination of fate and organizational design, the dynamic of the business over the years expanded to include multiple business lines that complement the original gift shop concept. Each of the children chose to pursue tertiary education and/or receive external experience in areas that were different but still important to the business—operations, strategy, and accounting. This provided a robust platform for each to exercise his/her influence unencumbered by the rivalry that sometimes occurs when successors' interests overlap. It also helps that Mr. Johnson remains involved to guide and direct his successors, albeit with a flexible enough grip to entertain innovative concepts.

***

Conversations about
The Successor's Decision

The decision to accept or steer away from accepting a leadership role in the family business should never be assumed, go unvoiced, or be taken lightly. It is a decision that requires long-term commitment and has far-reaching impacts—on not only the successor, but also the business owner and everyone invested in the outcome. To ensure that family and business relationships are maintained, the successor must understand and gracefully deal with the effects of their choice.

This chapter is provides the necessary tools for the successor to participate in the smooth transition of the business, regardless of whether they are accepting or rejecting the role.

Key conversations discussed in this chapter:

- **Scenario Eight:** I do not want to run the business; I am interested in having a role in it.

- **Scenario Nine:** I do not want to run the business; I am not interested in having a role in it.

Scenario Eight: I do not want to run the business; I am interested in having a role in it

<u>Why is this key conversation so important?</u>

It is important to understand why the proposed successor wants to remain with the company but not to take the leadership role. This conversation will provide insight both on the leadership role itself as well as into the desires of the proposed successor. It is important to understand the reason for the decision. If the foundation alignment conversation was successful, the reasons behind this decision should not be a surprise. However, the reasons should never be assumed. The potential successor should still clearly and explicitly state his decision and rationale so that an appropriate solution and way forward could be discussed. Possible reasons for declining the incumbency are:

First, the proposed successor may not feel ready to take the leadership role. This individual may feel that they will someday be ready for the role but right now they either have other priorities or underdeveloped skills. In this case, the business owner will need to consider the feasibility of bringing in new leadership temporarily until this individual is ready to assume the incumbency.

Second, the proposed successor may not have the ambition or drive to take on the leadership role. Instead, this individual may prefer a role with less responsibility but with job security. The business owner in this case may need to consider how to provide the individual with a job that balances responsibility with job security.

Finally, there may be conditions pertaining to the business operations or performance that represent high risk and cause for concern for anyone taking a leadership role. These could include illegal or unethical behavior, declining performance and internally disruptive politics. The proposed successor may feel unwilling or unable to take on these particular types of business problems. This conversation can provide invaluable information to the business owner on how the company is perceived and the type of skills that will ultimately be required to run it.

What could happen if the conversation does not take place?

If the business owner is unclear about the reasons behind this individual's decision to turn down the leadership position, he/she may incorrectly try to pressure or lobby the individual into accepting it anyway.

Additionally, the business owner may incorrectly place this individual in an alternative position within the company without understanding his/her desires and motivations. For example, if the business owner interprets the reluctance of this individual to take the leadership role as a lack of drive or motivation, then the business owner may recommend a low-growth but secure position. This could have disappointing consequences for the individual who seeks training for the leadership role in the future.

When is the best time for the conversation to take place?

This conversation could happen as soon after the business owner and the individual have the initial conversation about succession. It should occur as soon as the individual is clear about his or her position. This could be as soon as possible before or just after an unexpected offer is received for the role of incumbency. For the reasons stated above, it is important to have this conversation before resuming the search for a successor.

Scenario Nine: I do not want to run the business; I am not interested in having a role in it

<u>Why is this key conversation so important?</u>

The key question here is "why?"—why does this individual, who might have been a frontrunner for the role, not want to be part of the business? It is important for the business owner, as well as the individual under consideration, to understand the underlying reasons for this decision. The individual may have a perception of the viability of the company that is unknown to the business owner. He or she may have completely different interests, or there may be other underlying reasons in this individual's personal history that are problematic. Whatever the reasons may be, it is important that the owner and this individual reach an agreement about how to tell the story of the succession that is beneficial to the company, as well as honoring the privacy of the individual.

Additionally, it is important to be aware that there are many eyes watching from the outside: including other family members, employees, business partners, and the media. All of these factions will be asking questions about the change in presumed direction for the succession. It is essential that the business owner, the individual, and the person who ends up becoming the successor, share a common story that puts the business and everyone involved in the succession in the best light.

<u>What could happen if the conversation does not take place?</u>

If this conversation along with its associated agreements does not occur, then it is quite possible that alternative stories will circulate, both within the family and within the other factions directly and indirectly involved in the succession. This may have a negative effect on the ability to hire the best successor, who may be put off by contradictory statements from the owner and this individual.

As always, it is important to safeguard the reputation and legacy of the business. Contradictory, perhaps negative, stories can erode public perception and result in lost customers.

<u>When is the best time for the conversation to take place?</u>

This conversation could happen as soon after the owner and the individual have the initial conversation about succession. It should occur as soon as the individual is clear about his or her position. This could be as soon as possible before or just after an unexpected offer is received for the role of incumbency. For the reasons stated above, this conversation needs to occur before the search for the successor resumes.

Chapter Four: Performance

Consider the story of Brian, a fourth-generation supermarket owner, whose father's untimely death thrust him into the role of person-in-charge. Preferring to split his time between his luxury homes in the Caribbean, Brian's presence in the business and work approach are a stark departure from his father's who had physically opened the main supermarket himself every morning.

Recognizing that their styles differed significantly, Brian, like his father before him, relied on a council of a tight-knit group of relatives—peers who also owned supermarkets in the family's chain—for guidance and oversight. Therefore, despite the absence of his father, there was some comfort that the stability of the business was being closely monitored and guided by a trusted board of overseers who still commanded respect in the hierarchical and paternal society.

They, in effect, served as de facto father figures to continue the task of teaching Brian the ropes that his father was unable to complete. No major decision could be made without their input and, in many cases, they did not hesitate to use their veto power.

***

Conversations about Performance

Maintaining performance standards during and after a transition is critical for the reassurance and continued faith of investors, customers, and other family members in the business and the new successor. Dropped standards can be potentially devastating on employee morale and business performance, and so managing the sensitive conversations around training, performance standards and creative freedom are essential.

In this chapter, we provide comprehensive guidelines for a variety of critical performance management conversations that must be had to ensure the continued success of the business.

Key conversations discussed in this chapter:

- **Scenario Ten:** I am passing the business to multiple successors, each with a substantial role.
- **Scenario Eleven:** I need more support in this new role.
- **Scenario Twelve:** I have little freedom to execute because of your presence.
- **Scenario Thirteen:** You (successor) are underperforming.
- **Scenario Fourteen:** We need to innovate or the business will suffer.
- **Scenario Fifteen:** Your new vision will kill my business.
- **Scenario Sixteen:** This business is taking over my life.

Scenario Ten: I am passing the business to multiple successors, each with a substantial role

Why is this key conversation so important?

All previous conversations have been one-to-one conversations between the owner and a potential successor. In this conversation, the successors have been working in the business and have come together with the owner to discuss and clarify their individual and collective performance objectives. This group conversation, or series of group conversations, is critical in order to ensure that there is no confusion or ambiguity as the group of successors move forward with their key roles in the business.

Further, this conversation is intended to move the successors from thinking of themselves as individual contributors to seeing themselves as a unified, synergistic unit working together for the success of the business. In order to build a strong and cohesive group, these conversations should happen on a regular basis.

It may be difficult for successors to set operational boundaries for their area of operation especially if another family member is involved. A joint meeting with the owner could help with the guidance needed around this.

Regular joint meetings ensure that there is not the perception or an actual information imbalance between the owner and one or more successors. With open and transparent communication, all relevant members would receive information at the same time but may also have the benefit of jointly brainstorming and aligning on solutions to any issues.

Additionally, some owners have used the joint sessions to spur beneficial internal competition by having successors report on and defend the performance of their area against pre-defined performance indicators.

What could happen if the conversation does not take place?

If the successors do not have this collective conversation, then there is a risk of misunderstandings regarding roles and responsibilities. This and any type of confusion could have a negative impact on both the productivity and the quality of services of the company. It may also have an impact on relationships with vendors and customers who are at risk of receiving contradictory or insufficient information from the successors.

<u>When is the best time for the conversation to take place?</u>

This conversation should occur the moment multiple family members start working in substantial roles within the business. It will be one of a series of conversations as the successors work out the details of their individual roles and responsibilities as well as how they will best work together.

Scenario Eleven: I need more support in this new role.

Why is this key conversation so important?

Even though a successor may have been thoroughly vetted and a transition preparation plan executed, the preparation may be perceived by the successor as insufficient. There may still be gaps in the successor's knowledge and capabilities. These gaps are usually within the areas of informal communication and informal decision-making - processes that have not been, and perhaps cannot be, explicitly explained to the successor. The successor may need additional or a different kind of preparation than what was provided. Consequently, he/she may feel ill equipped for the role. This conversation is important for two reasons:

First, the owner may not be aware that the successor is struggling. This conversation will identify the areas where the successor feels that additional support is needed.

Second, there may be a difference in the business philosophy of the owner and successor. The owner may have a 'sink or swim' attitude toward the transition while the successor may feel that a protracted, high-contact transition would be best. This conversation will clarify what types of support, if any, the successor will receive.

What could happen if the conversation does not take place?

If the successor does not reach out for assistance in a timely manner then problems may go unresolved in the business, hampering operations. When this happens, confidence in the leadership capabilities of the successor and stakeholder confidence in the business may erode, affecting the business' performance.

When is the best time for the conversation to take place?

This conversation may have several iterations. The first iteration may happen as early as a few weeks into the successor's assumption of the leadership position. A delicate balance will be required between the successor's confidence in his/her abilities and his/her need for additional support. This balance will determine the frequency of these conversations.

Scenario Twelve: I have little freedom to execute because of your presence

<u>Why is this key conversation so important?</u>

The term 'helicopter parent' is used to describe the parent who takes an excessive and sometimes overprotective interest in their child's life. This is the scenario of an owner who exhibits an overly keen interest in the business operations even after the transition period is over.

Successful business operations depend on clearly defined roles and responsibilities as well as clearly defined chains of command. When a successor takes over responsibility for a business, changes because of a new management style are to be expected. This can be difficult for a business to adjust to even in the most favorable circumstances.

The already challenging transition can be hampered if the previous owner continues to stay involved in the business in an undisciplined way. When this happens, the employees, customers, and vendors may receive contradictory messages. It will be unclear to them where authority lies for decisions. As a result, they may fail to complete their roles while waiting for clarification of contradictory or ambiguous directions.

The purpose of this conversation between the successor and the past owner is to clarify their relationship as it relates to business operations. In this conversation, the successor will express concern about the seeming over-involvement of the previous owner and strive to minimize any involvement that may be contradictory or disruptive to the new ways of working in the business.

<u>What could happen if the conversation does not take place?</u>

If this conversation does not occur then the employees, customers, and vendors of the business will continue to receive contradictory information. This will result in confusion as these contradictory directions are followed or not followed. The result will be a decrease in responsiveness, productivity, and even quality if the internal controls of the business fall into disarray.

When is the best time for the conversation to take place?

Ideally, the conversation to align on ways of working between successor and previous owner should happen before roles are handed over. However, this conversation is positioned as an intervention. It should happen after a misunderstanding occurs because of the previous owner's interference in some aspect of the business' operations. There may have been previous complaints or disagreements between the past owner and the successor, but this particular conversation will differ in its intensity. It should focus on the specific interference but also refer to previous example(s).

Scenario Thirteen: You (successor) are underperforming

<u>Why is this key conversation so important?</u>

A change in leadership is always fraught with uncertainty, no matter how positively it is initially received. Vendors and customers are uncertain if there will be changes in the way that they interact with the business. The workforce is uncertain about these changes as well. Even the larger community — dependents who rely on the salaries of these employees — will be concerned about any future changes.

So, when the successor fails to meet the required expectations there is reason for deep concern. Vendors and customers may shift their business to competitors. As revenue declines, the workforce may be subject to retrenchment and redundancies. This in turn affects the community. Once this downward cycle begins, it is extremely difficult to turnaround and restore faith in the company.

It is important that as soon as these downward trends are identified, corrective action is taken. This conversation by the board of directors or now-retired owner with his/her successor is the first step in righting the ship. It will identify the sources of underperformance and determine the corrections that need to be made.

<u>What could happen if the conversation does not take place?</u>

Without this conversation, the company may enter a downward cycle from which it will be difficult to recover. The negative effects of this downward cycle include loss of vendors and customers, followed by the forced and/or unforced departure of the workforce. Indeed, if corrective actions are not taken, the company could decline to the point of bankruptcy and/or closure.

When is the best time for the conversation to take place?

Ideally, this conversation should occur before the outer signs of underperformance are visible to the public. The retired owner and the board of directors should be on the lookout for rumblings from inside the company and/or declining performance. These might include evidence of the following:

- Loss of one or more key customers, employees or vendors
- Uncharacteristic increases in costs
- Disruptions to operations
- Unplanned decreases in productivity
- Increases in customer complaints

This conversation should occur at the first sign(s) of any of these events.

Scenario Fourteen: We need to innovate or the business will suffer

<u>Why is this key conversation so important?</u>

Spurred by technology and a number of digital and operational advancements, the ways of working of many businesses have changed substantially over the years. This change has at times resulted in the disruption to and obsolescence of some companies and industries. Most companies that were founded many years ago have survived by reinventing themselves to remain current in the eyes of their customers.

Spurred by the popularity of the start-up culture or an eagerness to keep the business on the cutting edge of change regardless of its current performance, a family member might have new ideas that he/she would like to implement. Without this conversation, the family member could leave the family business and start the venture on his/her own, taking his capabilities and a potential lifeline for the business with him/her.

He/she also recognizes that approval and guidance from the owner is critical to getting buy-in from other key decision makers and, eventually, implementation of the idea. In this conversation, the family member is presenting his/her ideas and asking for approval and freedom to implement along with guidance when needed.

However, it should be recognized that new ideas could come from anywhere. The owner may also be the one challenging his or her successors to implement an idea that he or she may have read or heard about.

If this conversation does not happen, the family member may leave to implement the idea elsewhere, robbing the company of the benefit of the innovation. Alternately, if this conversation between the successor and the owner does not occur, then it will be difficult for the successor to get the support within the company needed for the changes to be successful.

<u>When is the best time for the conversation to take place?</u>

This conversation could occur whenever someone within the business would like to discuss introducing an innovation into the business. This could even be before the succession process has begun. Ideally, it should occur once the person has a complete understanding of the business' operations. However, too much knowledge about the business could actually be a barrier to the fresh eyes and open-minded thinking that is needed for innovations and new ideas to flourish. As a matter of fact, a culture of innovation that encourages brainstorming ways to improve the business on a regular basis should be a common occurrence among the family members.

Scenario Fifteen: Your new vision will kill my business

<u>Why is this key conversation so important?</u>

When someone creates a business from the ground up, she will have a strong vision of what she wants the business to become. It is one of the special joys of creating a business to see that vision come to fruition. It is therefore completely understandable for a previous owner (particularly if he or she also founded the business) to feel enormous distress when he/she sees that cherished vision taken in a completely different direction by a successor.

There are many reasons why the successor may not carry forward the vision of a previous owner. There may be a desire to modernize or to change the product lines. There may be an understandable desire to make an imprint on the culture by introducing a new logo or a new brand image. In all of these cases, the successor may be unaware of the attachment that the owner, as well as the entire organization, has to a particular way of doing business. The successor may be unaware of the emotional pain that may ensue.

In this conversation, the previous owner has a discussion with the successor regarding changes that the successor is attempting post-transition.

<u>What could happen if the conversation does not take place?</u>

If the successor is not told about the distress that the changes are causing, then he or she may meet with unexpected resistance and loss of productivity that cannot otherwise be explained. Individuals within the organization may harbor unspoken resentments. These resentments will show up in lowered levels of cooperation and productivity. Even customers and vendors may leave the business when ways of doing business have changed. Key employees may depart if they feel no longer valued. The particular tragedy for the successor is that, unless this conversation occurs, he/she may never fully understand the causes of the decline and may attempt corrective efforts that make things even worse.

When is the best time for the conversation to take place?

The time for this conversation is a delicate balance. The past owner will naturally want to give the successor time to settle in to the leadership position. Some change is to be expected and tolerated. The time for this conversation is typically after feedback arrives from several of the individuals in the business who are unhappy with the proposed changes. This provides the past owner with the additional perspective of multiple voices instead of just his or her own.

Scenario Sixteen: This business is taking over my life

<u>Why is this key conversation so important?</u>

Oftentimes, reality can be very different from perception. While a successor may assume to know what working in the family business will be like, it may be quite different once he or she actually starts working in the business in a meaningful way. This is also where the lines between family and business will most likely become blurred. On the one hand, while the casual communication style and ability to 'be oneself' might be appreciated, sometimes the overexposure of such close relationships could end up becoming overwhelming.

Family members may start to realize that they see each other too much and that there is little time to mentally relax and unwind from business affairs. It might be hard to let go of the employee/boss dynamic during family gatherings that eventually transition to business talk. Additionally, disagreements at home might be brought into the office and these may negatively affect morale and overall employee productivity. Personalities at home (e.g. the pushy aunt), might remain the same at the office and some members (e.g. the immature baby brother) might struggle to be regarded differently in the office regardless of reporting lines and professional competence.

Increasingly a family member may feel overwhelmed by continued business discussions that are permeating into every aspect of his/her day-to-day life. This conversation is necessary to set boundaries that will allow the successor to relax and have some much-needed mental downtime.

<u>What could happen if the conversation does not take place?</u>

If other family members are not aware of the impact of their actions or that the successor is feeling overwhelmed, the seeming intrusions into his or her personal life will continue. The successor would be at risk of burning out and resenting these intrusions. This may spur a negative spiral of rebellious behavior, either at home or at work, which could be damaging to business and personal relationships. In some cases, family members have even left the family business to create the separation that they need to function at their best.

<u>When is the best time for the conversation to take place?</u>

This conversation should happen in a period of calm as soon as possible after the successor recognizes that he or she needs some space but before he or she reaches a breaking point. Ahead of the discussion, the successor should determine what he or she requires in order to create the needed separation. For example, no business talk at the dinner table or no family 'pet names' at the office. This conversation could happen either one on one with the offending family member, or with the entire family for a more general issue.

Chapter Five: The Exit

Mr. Willis owned and ran the biggest and most successful wholesale company in the city. We would chat from time to time. A gentleman in his late-sixties, he was well known and respected by multinational conglomerates for the growth that his business afforded their products. The business ran smoothly under his watchful eye. Before the doors opened at eight, Mr. Willis could be found on the premises at six o'clock every morning, feeding the birds as he started his day. When the doors opened, he took his seat in a place that offered the best view of the comings and goings of employees and customers, barking orders into an old cell phone of the pre-smartphone era. He was as old-school as they come.

He came from nothing and, with little formal education and a family to support, he did his best to figure things out. He built the business brick by brick. "I am self-taught," he would beam proudly. "And all of my kids are doctors."

All of his children received their Ivy League educations fully funded and paid for by the success of the business. "Things aren't like they used to be before. What would they do with a business like this? I am setting them up so that they can do their own thing," he would say with a tinge of wistfulness. And he was right. With no one groomed to take over the business, he was enjoying what would most likely be the end of its heyday. A business like his relies more on relationships and street-smarts than it does book-smarts.

I would always inquire about his good friend, Chris, who similarly owned a successful logistics business that had provided well for his wife, Valerie, and their children, who had then gone off to follow their dreams. "Oh, they're complaining that the house is getting too big," he would lament with a smile. "You know that Valerie redid the kitchen again."

This would be the second gut renovation of the kitchen in four years for a couple who were enjoying the spoils of their labour. Another prominent businessman, another strong conglomerate with no succession plan.

***

Conversations about The Exit

There are many reasons why a family must consider the closure of the family business. Given the intense emotional and financial, implications of such a decision, how this conversation is approached must be handled with professionalism, patience and a tremendous empathy and understanding.

In this chapter, we explore the conversations from the perspective of both the owner and the successor, ensuring that this critical decision is managed effectively while keeping the family relationships intact.

Key conversations discussed in this chapter:

- o **Scenario Seventeen:** I am selling the business.
- o **Scenario Eighteen:** You should sell the business.

Scenario Seventeen: I am selling the business

<u>Why is this key conversation so important?</u>

Preparing for a business' succession is not something that happens in a day or a week; it happens over years and sometimes decades. When the owner decides to sell the company, there are many individuals, including one or more potential successors, whose lives are affected. Selling a company, especially a family-run company, also carries with it emotional connotations that extend through the family, the workforce, and the larger community. This conversation between the owner and a potential successor will clarify how the sales process will proceed, the options that are possible, as well as how to orchestrate communications with multiple individuals and groups.

<u>What could happen if the conversation does not take place?</u>

Without this conversation, there will be a great deal of anxiety across all of the impacted individuals and groups. Family members will be uncertain of what, if any, benefits they will receive, workforce members will be uncertain of their future employment, and the community will be uncertain of its economic future, as will the potential successor and other key executives. This conversation is essential to answering these questions and allaying associated fears.

<u>When is the best time for the conversation to take place?</u>

This conversation should occur before the sale is announced. It should be a private conversation between the owner and any key stakeholder or prominent family members and it should establish the parameters for the sale.

Scenario Eighteen: You should sell the business

<u>Why is this key conversation so important?</u>

This conversation is between the owner and a representative of the stakeholders who wish to encourage the sale of the family business. There are many reasons why the stakeholders in a family business may decide that it is time to have this discussion. These include:

- The declining health of the owner and the absence of viable successor(s)
- The products and/or services that the company sells may no longer be relevant and/or profitable
- Increased costs of operation may be eroding profits

Whatever the reason, it is important for the owner and the stakeholder(s) to reach a consensus regarding how to proceed. This may be made difficult by the owner's emotional and sentimental attachment to the business even when it has survived long past its prime. For this reason, a face-to-face, discussion is required that balances fact with empathy.

Family members should balance the practical need to sell the business with the human need of the owner to find meaning in life by doing work that he or she has done the majority of his life. If closing the business may have a worse impact on the wellbeing of the owner, then it may be worthwhile to explore other options.

<u>What could happen if the conversation does not take place?</u>

If such a discussion does not occur, there may be a tendency on the owner's part to delay the painful decision to sell. Postponing the inevitable may continue to put the owner's health in jeopardy and may further erode the salability of the business and the options that are available to the stakeholders, including the family, workforce, and community a whole.

<u>When is the best time for the conversation to take place?</u>

The best time to have such a discussion is immediately following the receipt of a doctor's recommendation or the close of a business's fiscal year. The end of the fiscal year is the time when the most comprehensive picture of the true state of the company is available.

Conclusion

Family businesses are a special, and critical, part of our economy. There are thousands of businesses that fall under this category and thousands more nuances that come with each unique dynamic. The conversations in this book are designed to act as guidelines that will equip you to begin successfully navigating your succession plan.

Succession Strength, Inc. is a company devoted to ensuring the transition between leaders is smooth, prosperous and helps family relationships thrive. With the help of our organizational psychologist, we have created a detailed conversation guide for each of the scenarios discussed in this book. Assess your business' communication strength at www.SuccessionStrength.com/assessment. Visit us for additional tools, information, or a custom solution for navigating your succession journey.

Our Framework

To avoid succession stress and ensure succession strength, the Succession Strength approach is built on three pillars—Communication, Preparation and Execution.

Communication forms the basis of the framework and runs throughout the Preparation and Execution phases. In our work, we have found that a number of key conversations are missing, overlooked or given too little attention in the succession process. Ineffective communication often results in a misalignment of objectives and stress that often results in the failure of the business.

For this reason, we focus in depth on the key conversations that should be had before, during and after a business transition from the perspective of both the business owner and the successor. Communication was the focus of this book. For more in-depth help with tricky conversations, harness the power of our organizational psychologist. Download one of our step-by-step conversation guides.

Preparation focuses on protecting the existing business while putting the correct measures in place to anticipate and survive the upcoming change.

Execution brings the phases together and builds on the work done in the Communication and Preparation pillars.

Our Succession Strength Assessment helps businesses assess their succession readiness and overcome transition hurdles related to Communication, Preparation and Execution. Assess your businesses' succession readiness at www.successionstrength.com/assessment.

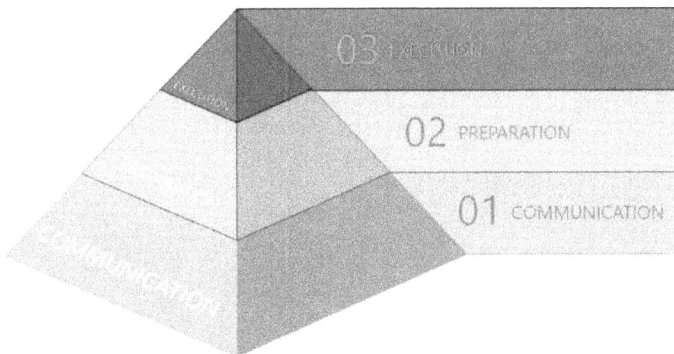

About The Author

Global strategist, **Rochelle Clarke**, is founder and CEO of Succession Strength. Complementing her MBA from University of Pennsylvania's Wharton School of Business, Rochelle brings nearly twenty years of strategy experience to Succession Strength, the practice she founded to help businesses overcome barriers to smooth succession transitions. Balancing strategic thinking and operational practicality, she has worked with businesses of all sizes in a variety of countries combining a variety of best practices and practical solutions to enable success.

Rochelle is Content Director of Succession Strength's solutions created by her team of organizational psychology and business experts.

Want more?

For more in-depth help with tricky conversations, harness the power of our organizational psychologist. Download one of our step by step conversation guides. Assess your businesses' succession readiness at
www.successionstrength.com/assessment

If you found this book helpful, we would love to hear from you! Email us at info@SuccessionStrength.com to let us know how we could serve you better.

Connect with the Succession Strength team for the latest news and updates!

Website: www.SuccessionStrength.com
Facebook and Instagram: @SuccessionStrength
Twitter: @SuccessionStre1
LinkedIn: SuccessionStrength
Medium

www.ingramcontent.com/pod-product-compliance
Lightning Source LLC
Chambersburg PA
CBHW060507220326
41598CB00025B/3592